DANGEROUS JOBS
SEARCH AND RESCUE

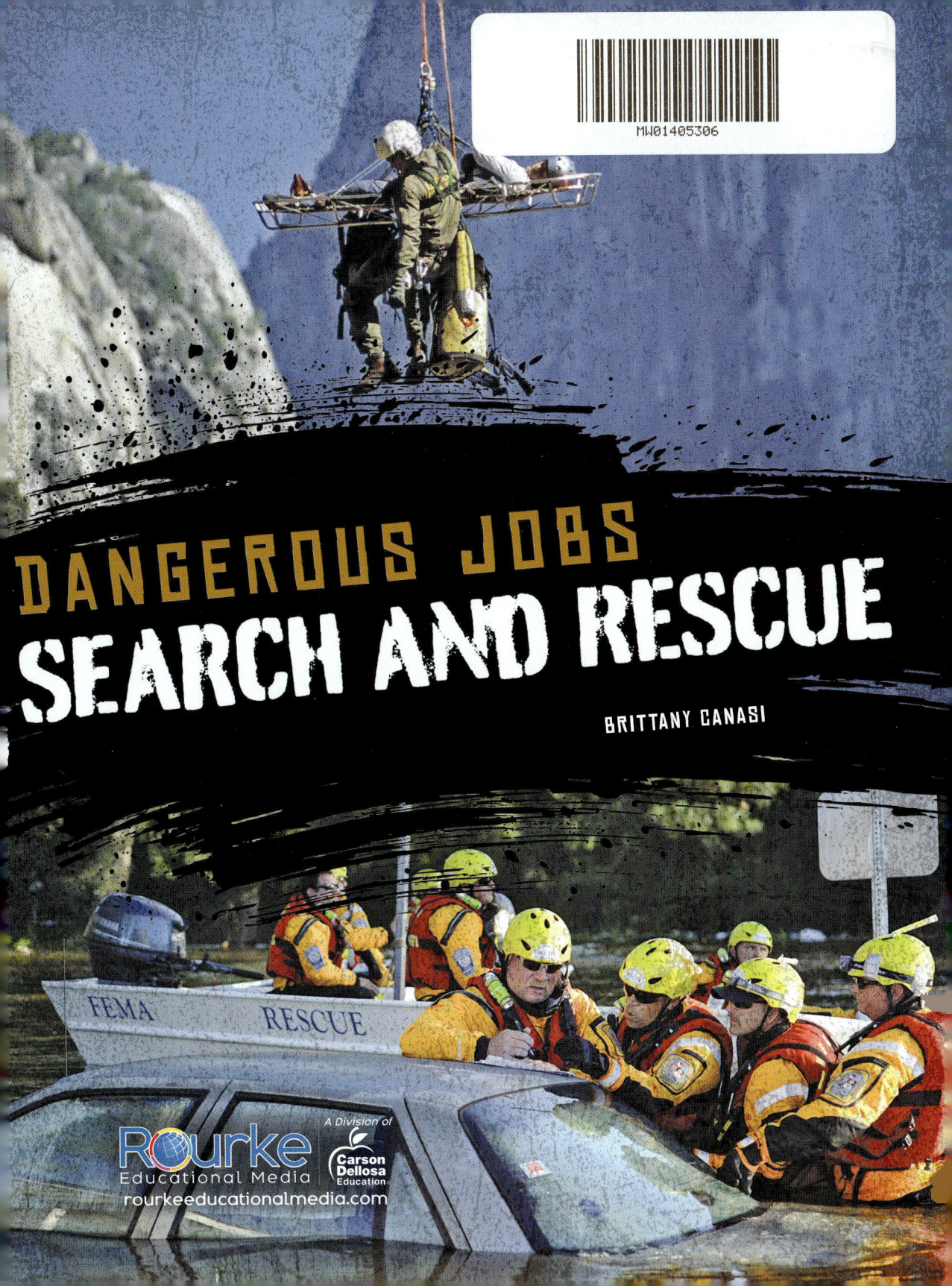

BRITTANY CANASI

ROURKE'S SCHOOL to HOME CONNECTIONS
BEFORE AND DURING READING ACTIVITIES

Before Reading: *Building Background Knowledge and Vocabulary*

Building background knowledge can help children process new information and build upon what they already know. Before reading a book, it is important to tap into what children already know about the topic. This will help them develop their vocabulary and increase their reading comprehension.

Questions and Activities to Build Background Knowledge:

1. Look at the front cover of the book and read the title. What do you think this book will be about?
2. What do you already know about this topic?
3. Take a book walk and skim the pages. Look at the table of contents, photographs, captions, and bold words. Did these text features give you any information or predictions about what you will read in this book?

Vocabulary: *Vocabulary Is Key to Reading Comprehension*

Use the following directions to prompt a conversation about each word.

- Read the vocabulary words.
- What comes to mind when you see each word?
- What do you think each word means?

Vocabulary Words:
- combat
- remote
- scuba dive
- topography
- urban
- wilderness

During Reading: *Reading for Meaning and Understanding*

To achieve deep comprehension of a book, children are encouraged to use close reading strategies. During reading, it is important to have children stop and make connections. These connections result in deeper analysis and understanding of a book.

Close Reading a Text

During reading, have children stop and talk about the following:

- Any confusing parts
- Any unknown words
- Text to text, text to self, text to world connections
- The main idea in each chapter or heading

Encourage children to use context clues to determine the meaning of any unknown words. These strategies will help children learn to analyze the text more thoroughly as they read.

When you are finished reading this book, turn to the next-to-last page for **After Reading Questions** and an **Activity**.

Table of Contents

Rescue Needed. 4
Wilderness and Water. 12
Combat Rescue 24
Memory Game 30
Index 31
After Reading Questions 31
Activity 31
About the Author 32

Rescue Needed

A lost hiker. A hurt boater.
A trapped child. They all must
be rescued.

Search and rescue teams work in **remote** areas. They work in cities too. They work in any weather.

Local Leaders

Local sheriffs lead many of these teams. Some large parks have their own teams.

remote (ri-MOHT): far away in time or space; secluded or isolated

Tornadoes. Wildfires. Floods. Collapsed bridges and buildings. FEMA's **urban** search and rescue teams help people in disasters.

What is FEMA?

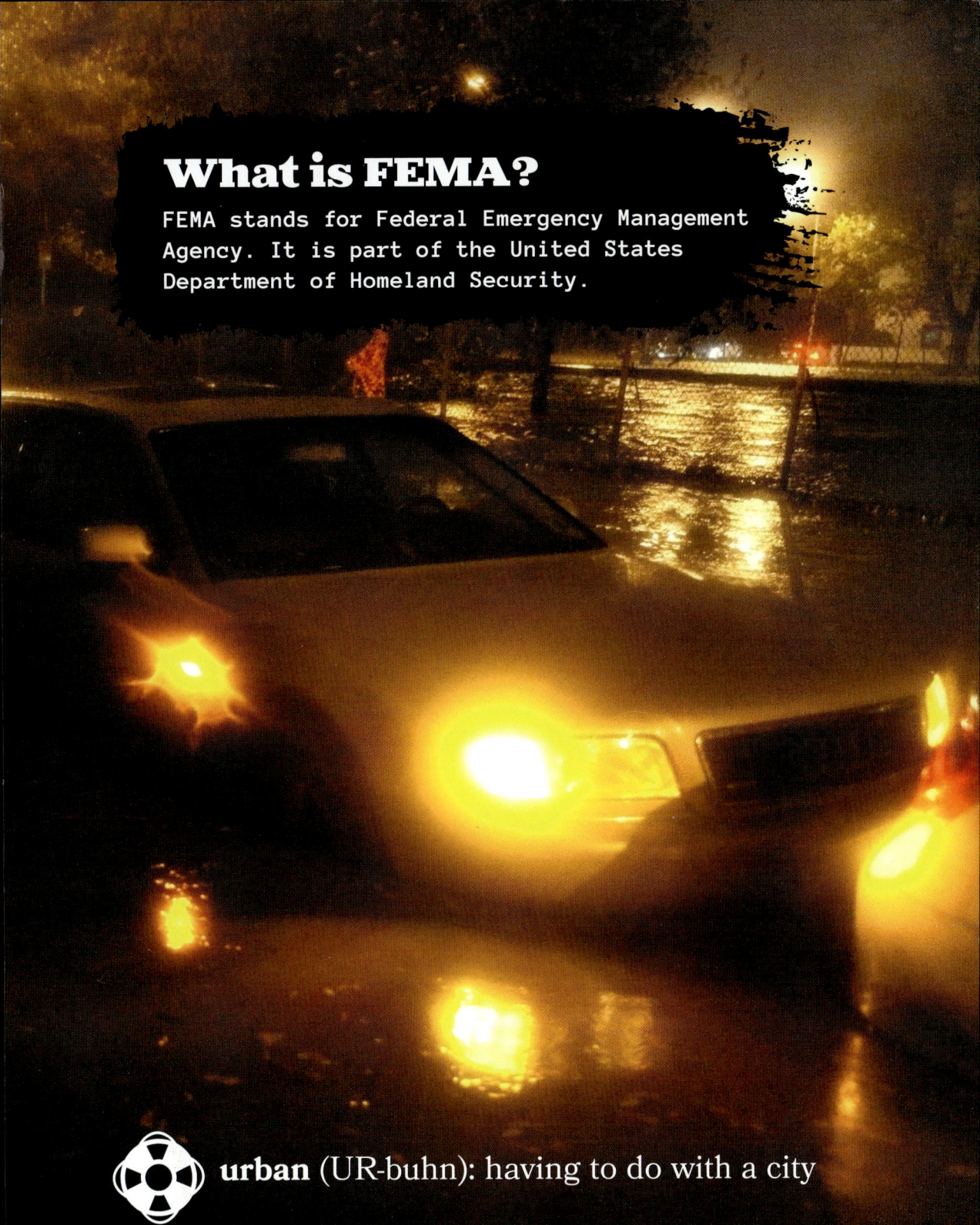

FEMA stands for Federal Emergency Management Agency. It is part of the United States Department of Homeland Security.

urban (UR-buhn): having to do with a city

Urban search and rescue takes place in tight spaces, such as collapsed buildings. Electrical wires, broken gas lines, and unstable structures add to the danger.

11

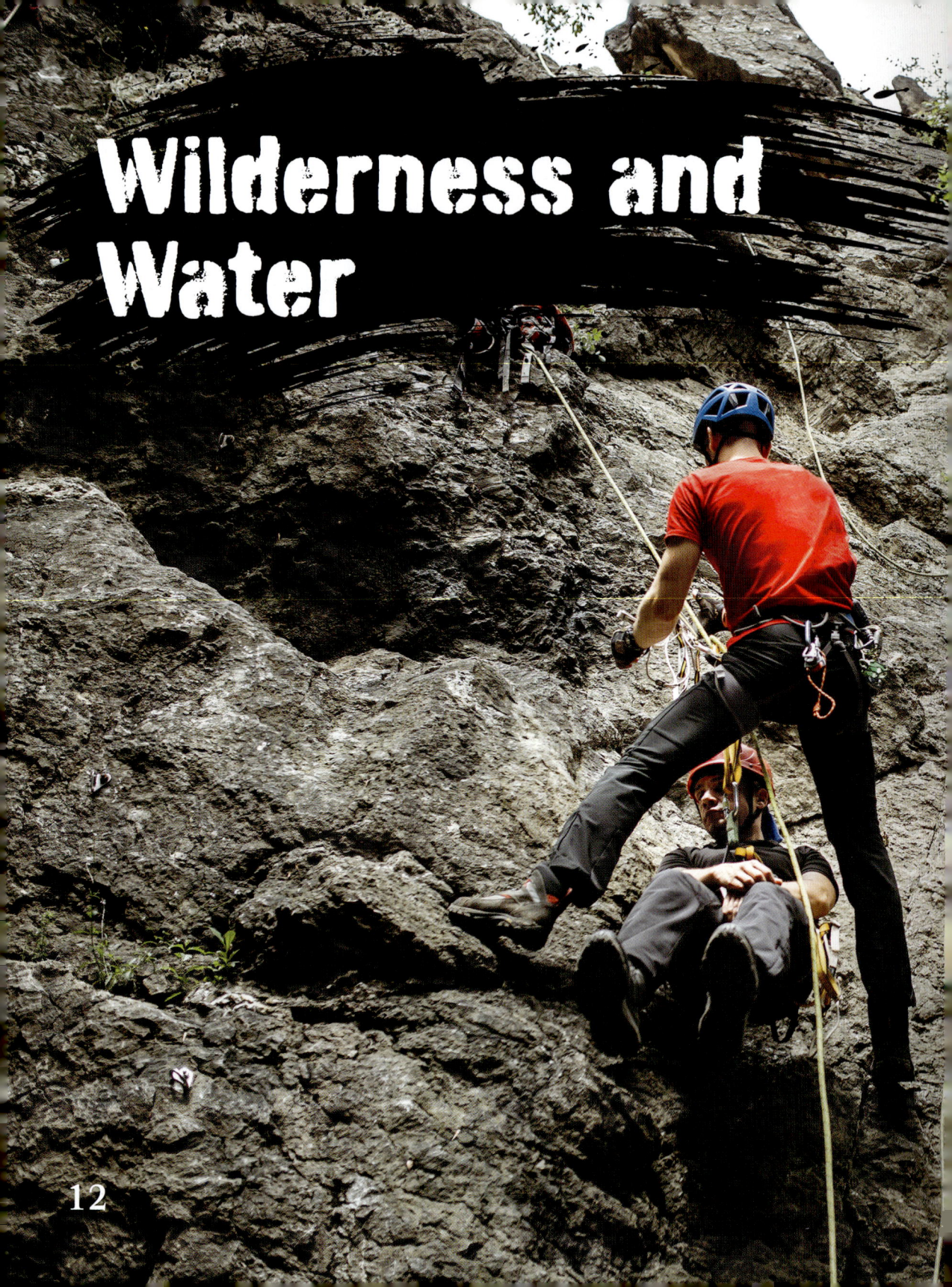

Wilderness and Water

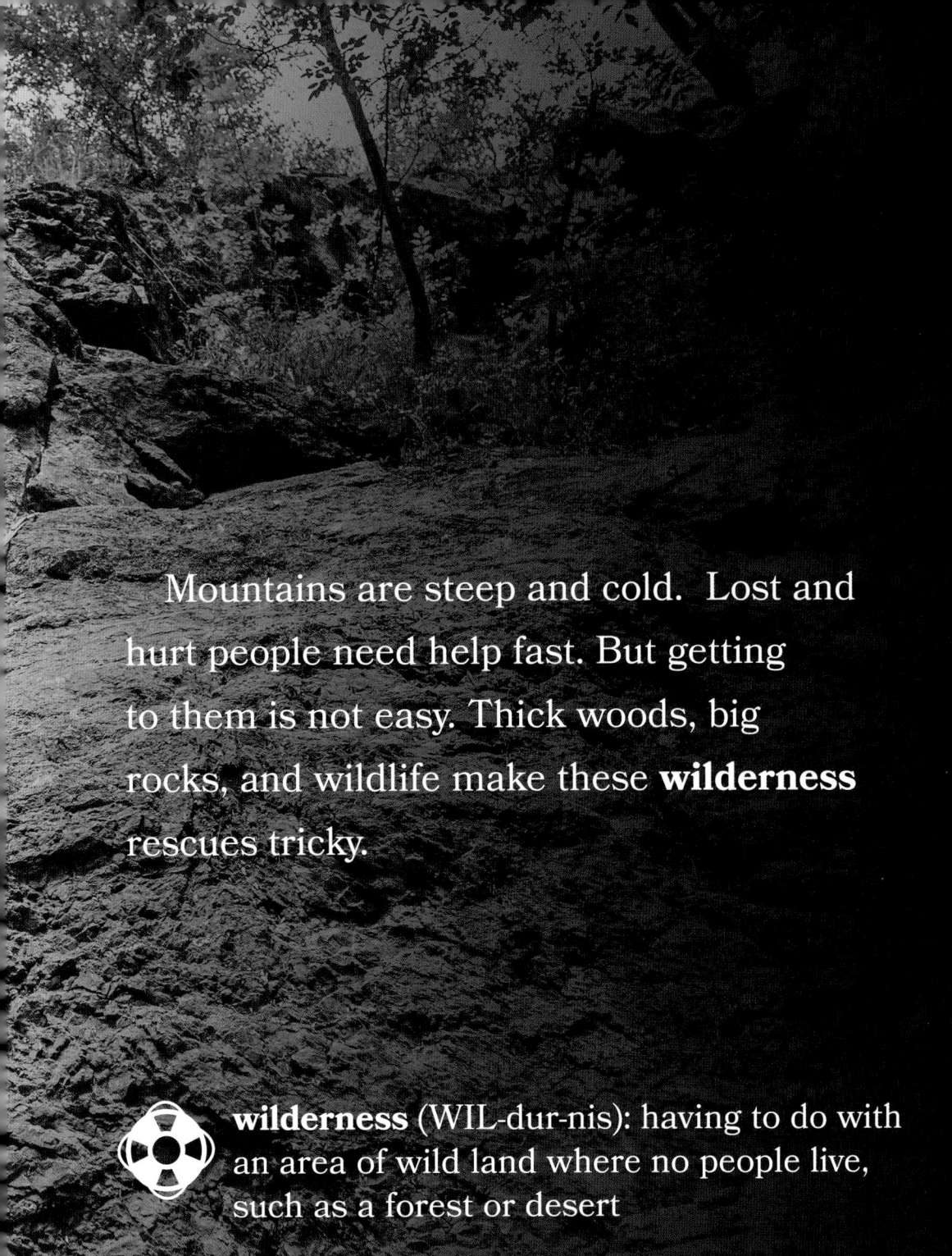

Mountains are steep and cold. Lost and hurt people need help fast. But getting to them is not easy. Thick woods, big rocks, and wildlife make these **wilderness** rescues tricky.

wilderness (WIL-dur-nis): having to do with an area of wild land where no people live, such as a forest or desert

Mountain rescuers have wilderness training. They know how to read **topography** maps. They may have tracking and search skills.

topography (tuh-PAH-gruh-fee): having to do with the detailed description of the physical features of an area including hills, valleys, mountains, fields, rivers, and lakes

Daring Dogs

Rescue dogs help many rescue teams. These dogs can find people lost in the woods or trapped in fallen buildings.

Mountain Money

Mountain rescue is usually free, but not in Switzerland. A rescue in the Swiss Alps could cost nearly four thousand dollars!

One rescuer crashed his helicopter on the way to help a mountain climber. He left the crash and walked the rest of the way. The climber was saved!

17

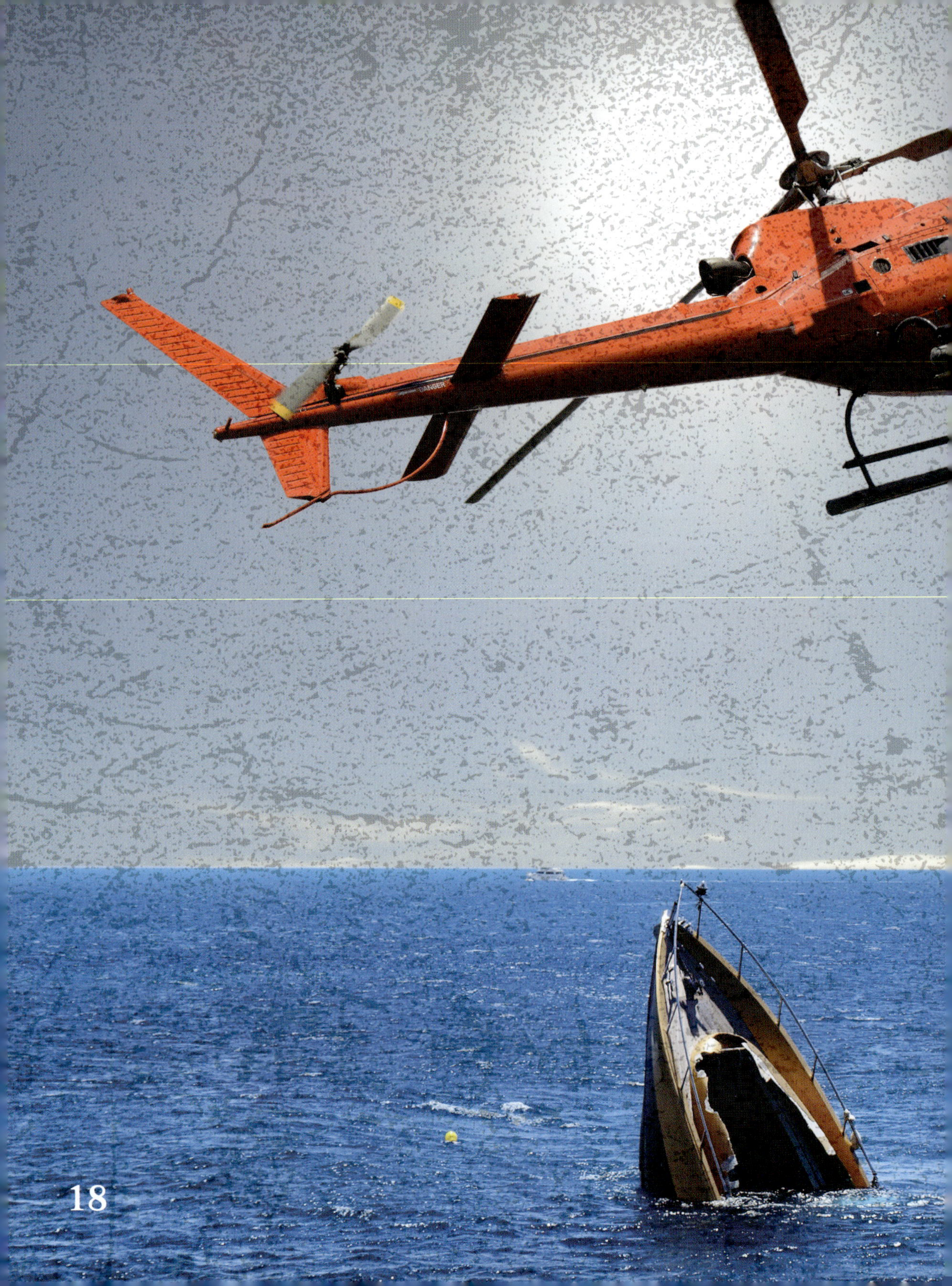
DANGER

Sinking boats and other accidents call for water rescues. In the United States, the U.S. Coast Guard handles most of these rescues.

Trained rescue swimmers must swim in freezing, rough water. They must be skilled and strong.

Elite Team

There are only about 300 rescue swimmers in the Coast Guard. They stay in rough seas for up to 30 minutes. They practice making decisions while waves crash over them.

A cave's location, depth, water level, and temperature can affect a rescue plan. Cave rescuers have water and mountain rescue skills. They also know how to fight fires.

Cave Crisis

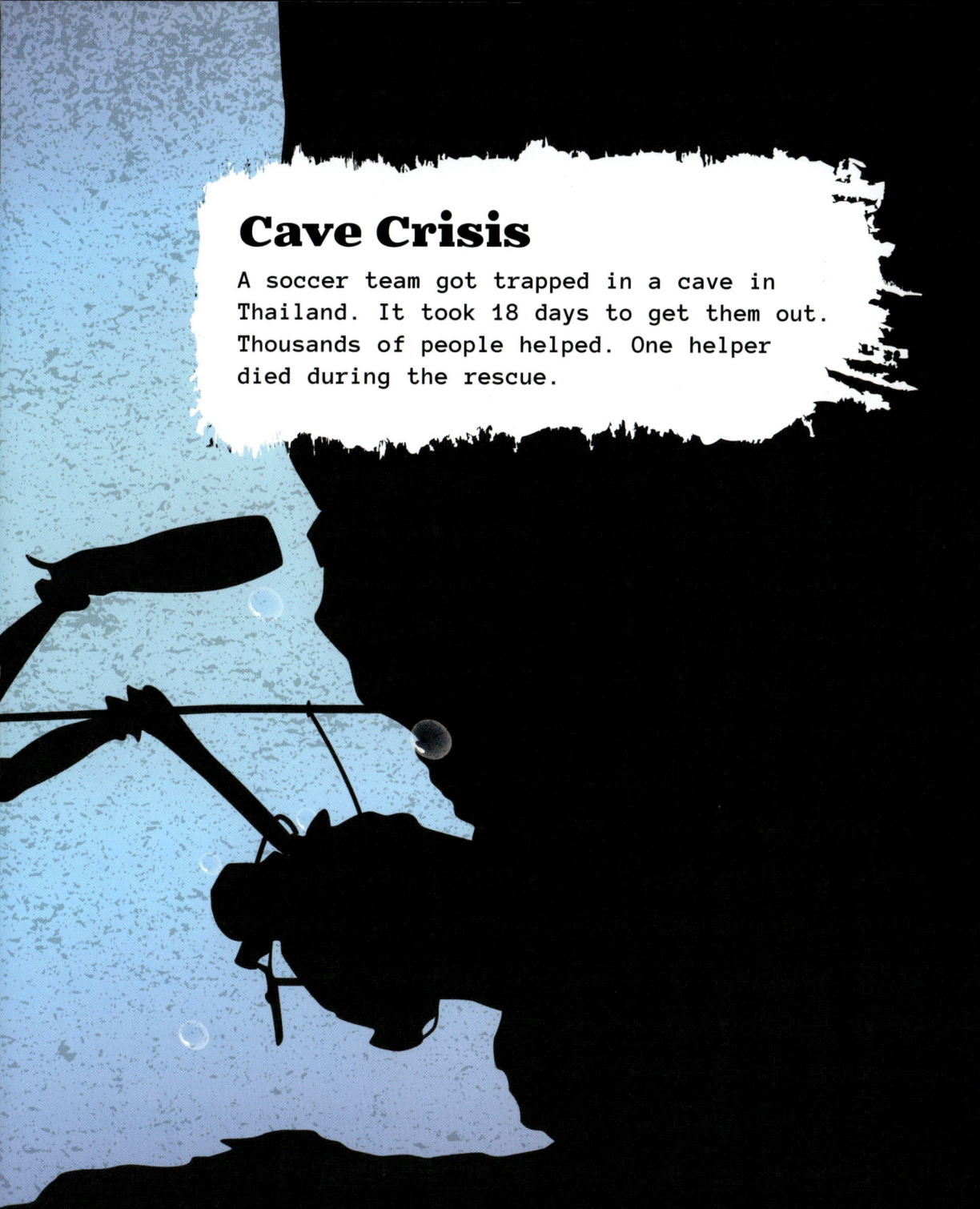

A soccer team got trapped in a cave in Thailand. It took 18 days to get them out. Thousands of people helped. One helper died during the rescue.

Combat Rescue

Soldiers can get hurt, lost, or trapped. Some teams are trained in **combat** rescue. Soldiers trained in combat rescue are called Combat Rescue Officers, or CROs.

combat (KAHM-bat): having to do with fighting between people or armies

Combat rescuers are skilled in the air and the water. They can **scuba dive**. They can parachute. They also have first aid skills.

scuba dive (SKOO-bah dive): to swim underwater using a tank of compressed air that is breathed through a hose; *scuba* is short for *self-contained underwater breathing apparatus*

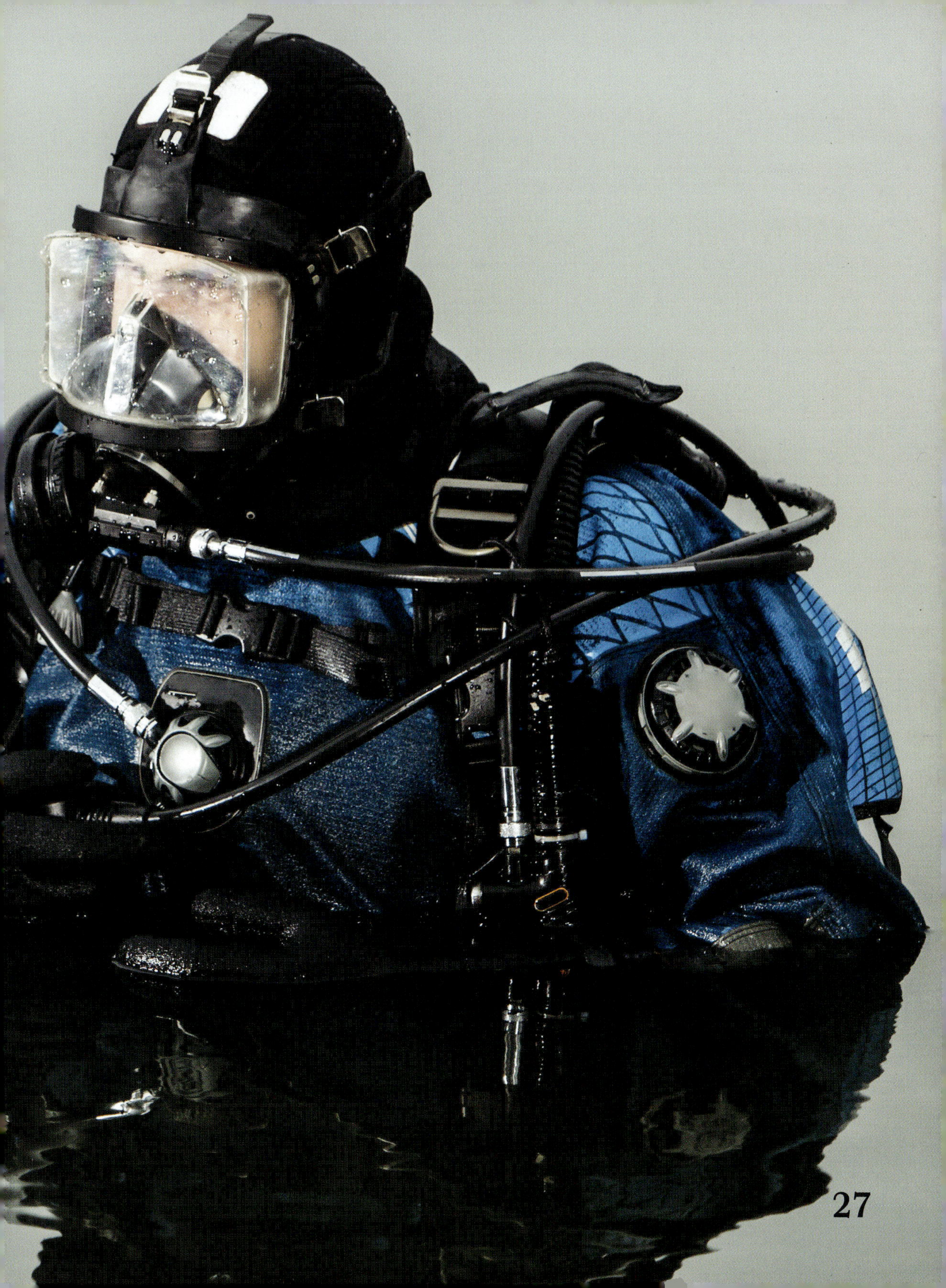

Combat rescuers use aircraft with special equipment. Some can lower beds for hurt soldiers. Some can refuel other aircraft in mid-air.

Daring Helpers

Search and rescue teams risk their lives to help others get to safety.

Memory Game

Look at the pictures. What do you remember reading on the pages where each image appeared?

30

Index

aircraft 28
cave 22, 23
disasters 8
equipment 28

mountain(s) 13, 14, 16, 17, 22
soldiers 24
tracking 14
water 12, 19, 20, 22, 26

After Reading Questions

1. Where could you be charged for a mountain rescue?
2. What are some possible dangers in urban search and rescue?
3. Which agency leads most water rescues?
4. What is a CRO and what do they do?
5. About how many rescue swimmers are in the United States Coast Guard?

Activity

Imagine a hiker is injured on a remote trail. How would you rescue them? Use the internet or books to research different ways that the hiker could be found and helped.

About the Author

Brittany Canasi's job is in cartoons, and her passion is in writing. Brittany has a B.A. in creative writing from Florida State University, and she lives in Los Angeles with her husband and very scruffy dogs. When she's not writing, she enjoys hiking and hopes she never has to be rescued.

© 2020 Rourke Educational Media

All rights reserved. No part of this book may be reproduced or utilized in any form or by any means, electronic or mechanical including photocopying, recording, or by any information storage and retrieval system without permission in writing from the publisher.

www.rourkeeducationalmedia.com

PHOTO CREDITS: Cover & Title Page ©MichaelSvoboda, ©sierrarat; Pg 3, 10 18, 23, 30, 32 ©ulimi; Pg 7 ©ZullU InFocus; Pg 8 ©FashionStock.com; Pg 10 ©hxdbzxy; Pg 14 ©Rainer Lesniewski; Pg 18 ©Lisa-Blue; Pg 20 ©CarlKemp; Pg 26 © Aleksandr Tsybulskyy; Pg 28 ©burtika; Pg 15 & 30 ©wpohldesign; Pg 16 & 30 ©thamerpic; Pg 22 & 30 ©Nicole Rerk; Pg 24 & 30 ©Lorado; Pg 4 & 30 ©MichaelSvoboda; Pg 12 & 30 ©astarot; Pg 3, 4, 12, 24, 30, 31, 32 ©sierrarat; Pg 30 ©Dimasu

Edited by: Kim Thompson
Cover design by: Rhea Magaro-Wallace
Interior design by: Kathy Walsh

Library of Congress PCN Data

Search and Rescue / Brittany Canasi
(Dangerous Jobs)
ISBN 978-1-73161-509-1 (hard cover)
ISBN 978-1-73161-316-5 (soft cover)
ISBN 978-1-73161-614-2 (e-Book)
ISBN 978-1-73161-719-4 (ePub)
Library of Congress Control Number: 2019932154

Rourke Educational Media
Printed in the United States of America,
North Mankato, Minnesota